Helping Dogs

WORKING ✿ DOGS

By Mary Ann Hoffman

Gareth Stevens
Publishing

Please visit our Web site, www.garethstevens.com. For a free color catalog of all our high-quality books, call toll free 1-800-542-2595 or fax 1-877-542-2596.

Library of Congress Cataloging-in-Publication Data

Hoffman, Mary Ann, 1947-
Helping dogs / Mary Ann Hoffman.
    p. cm. — (Working dogs)
Includes index.
ISBN 978-1-4339-4652-3 (pbk.)
ISBN 978-1-4339-4653-0 (6-pack)
ISBN 978-1-4339-4651-6 (library binding)
1. Service dogs. I. Title.
HV1569.6.H64 2011
362.4'0483—dc22

2010035242

First Edition

Published in 2011 by
Gareth Stevens Publishing
111 East 14th Street, Suite 349
New York, NY 10003

Copyright © 2011 Gareth Stevens Publishing

Designer: Michael J. Flynn
Editor: Kristen Rajczak

Photo credits: Cover, pp. 1, 13, 14, 18, 20 Shutterstock.com; p. 5 Dominique Faget/ AFP/Getty Images; p. 6 Huntstock/Getty Images; p. 9 Erik S. Lesser/Getty Images; p. 10 Thinkstock.com; p. 17 iStockphoto.com.

Printed in the United States of America

CPSIA compliance information: Batch #CR214250GS: For further information contact Gareth Stevens, New York, New York at 1-800-542-2595.

Contents

Words in the glossary appear in **bold** type the first time they are used in the text.

Helping Dogs

Helping dogs are working dogs. They are trained to **assist** people who need help with everyday tasks. They are taught special skills to be useful. Helping dogs are trained to pay attention. They are loving. They are gentle with strangers. Helping dogs are smart, **loyal**, and obey commands. Helping dogs are very important to many people. We will look at two types of helping dogs—service dogs and **therapy** dogs.

Dog Tales

Service dogs are allowed by law to go into places that other dogs are not, such as restaurants, buses, and airplanes.

◁ This service dog is on duty!

5

Dog Tales

Service dogs are not pets. They are trained to meet special needs. Some can even understand sign language!

This dog knows a special way to open the door. ▷

Service Dogs

Service dogs are trained to do special tasks that help people lead more independent lives. Service dogs are chosen for their size, **nature**, and ability to learn. Some guide people who cannot see. Some can open doors. Some can bring things to people. Some help people who cannot hear. They listen for certain sounds and let their owners know when the sound happens—a telephone or doorbell ringing, or even a baby crying. Some service dogs even push wheelchairs!

Learning the Job

Training service dogs requires time and special exercises. Assistance dogs are taught **physical** tasks their owners need help with. The dogs learn not to pay attention to anything but their job. Guide dogs for the blind learn to lead their owner safely. They cross streets, take stairs, and go under low-hanging objects. Service dogs for the **deaf** are taught to go to a sound and back to their owner. They let their owner know where the sound is coming from.

Many service dogs start training as puppies.

9

Golden **retrievers** are quick learners. They love having a job to do!

Golden Retrievers

Many **breeds** can be trained as service dogs. Golden retrievers are powerful, smart, and calm. Because of their size, golden retrievers should wear a **harness**. This makes it easier to handle them. Since they are not too big, golden retrievers fit well into most public places. Golden retrievers are quiet and easygoing. Their good nature and how they act around people in unfamiliar settings make them ideal assistance dogs.

Labrador Retrievers

Labrador retrievers are dependable, friendly, and helpful. They like to find and bring back objects. They have very soft mouths and can hold objects without breaking them. They learn quickly. These features make them ideal assistance dogs. Labs can be trained to turn lights on and off, open and close doors, and bring and remove objects. They help their owners balance as they walk and go for help when there is danger.

Dog Tales

Labs have even been taught to help their owners use bank machines.

This yellow lab is ready to help its owner do things that may be hard for him.

13

Dog Tales

There are lists of trained therapy dogs in communities. This makes finding a therapy dog and contacting its owner easy.

Therapy dogs make friends with everyone, especially people who are sick or lonely.

Therapy Dogs

Therapy dogs and their owners visit hospitals, homes for older people, special schools, and other places. They come in all breeds and sizes. They are friendly, gentle, and have easy natures. Therapy dogs are trained to obey commands. Their training is not as specific as service dog training because their purpose is different. Therapy dogs do not help only one person with daily tasks. Their job is to give love and comfort to many people.

Training to Help

Therapy dogs and their **handlers** train together. The handler is usually the dog's owner. The owners **volunteer** their dogs. The dogs are trained to accept petting and attention from many people. They obey their handler's commands. They learn how to behave in different settings and stay calm. Dogs and handlers go on planned visits. Both the dogs and the handlers enjoy going to different places to help people.

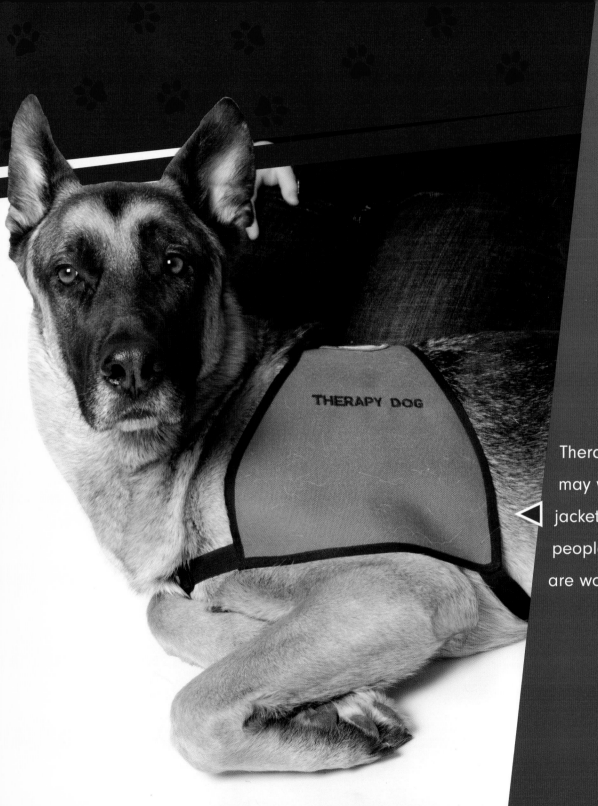

Therapy dogs may wear colorful jackets or vests so people know they are working.

Dog Tales

The Cavalier King Charles spaniel is named after King Charles II of England.

Cavalier King Charles spaniels are called "toy dogs." They are only about 12 inches (30 cm) high. They weigh less than 20 pounds (9 kg).

18

Cavalier King Charles Spaniels

The Cavalier King Charles spaniel makes an excellent therapy dog. It is very friendly to people and other dogs. It is playful, has a gentle nature, and likes to please. Cavalier King Charles spaniels are smart and easily trained. They are also very loyal. These dogs are small. Most people are not afraid of them because of their size. Taking these dogs from place to place is simple.

Making Life Better

Helping dogs make life better for people. They are attentive, loving, gentle, trustworthy, and loyal. Helping dogs provide a great service to individuals and communities. They act as eyes, ears, and hands for some people. They bring friendship, happiness, and comfort to others.

Jobs for Helping Dogs

Service Dog	Therapy Dog
trained to assist people who need help with daily tasks	**trained to give love and comfort to the lonely and sick**
guide the blind and people who do not see well	visit hospitals, schools for people with learning problems, nursing homes
locate sounds for the deaf and people who do not hear well	spend time with older people and people who are alone
assist people who have limited movement	provide support for people in hard situations

Glossary

assist: help

breed: a group of animals that share features different from other groups of the kind

deaf: not able to hear

handler: a person who trains and controls an animal

harness: straps used to control an animal

loyal: faithful

nature: the way someone or something acts

physical: using the body

retriever: a dog who goes to get—or retrieve—game for a hunter

therapy: treatment

volunteer: to offer to do a job without payment

For More Information

Books:

Hall, Becky. *Morris and Buddy: The Story of the First Seeing Eye Dog.* Morton Grove, IL: Albert Whitman & Company, 2007.

McDaniel, Melissa. *Guide Dogs.* New York, NY: Bearport Publishing, 2005.

Miller, Marie-Therese. *Helping Dogs.* New York, NY: Chelsea Clubhouse, 2007.

Web Sites:

American Kennel Club for Juniors and Kids
www.akc.org/kids_juniors
Find pictures and facts about dog breeds.

Woof! It's a Dog's Life
www.pbs.org/wgbh/woof/
Read training tips, stories, and play a trivia game as you learn about dogs.

Publisher's note to educators and parents: Our editors have carefully reviewed these Web sites to ensure that they are suitable for students. Many Web sites change frequently, however, and we cannot guarantee that a site's future contents will continue to meet our high standards of quality and educational value. Be advised that students should be closely supervised whenever they access the Internet.

Index